PRIZE W [barcode] Leadership

for the Social Sector

Do Something NEW To Win Your PRIZE

Roger Fairhead

Foreword by Danny Flynn (YMCA)

ISBN: 9781726666244

DEDICATION

To my wife Sue, and my children Adam and Amanda,

who inspire me to be all that I can be.

Roger Fairhead

Foreword

I have known Roger for over 15 years; almost as long as I have been CEO of the YMCA in North Staffordshire. I was excited when Roger joined the board and he was soon appointed as Vice Chair. Unfortunately though, due to Rogers business pressures at the time, he was unable continue in that role, however, in that time I got to know Roger as a bright able man who had a depth of knowledge and skills manifest so clearly in his book "PRIZE Winning Leadership".

The debate around leadership and management rages in both academic and business circles. Production managers want more efficiency, while people leaders want more effectiveness. People often argue from an absolute position of "either/or", when what we really want is "both/and ". Let me give you an example from the YMCA. When I got here its culture and practise was very administrative, and full of rules and procedures, often (in my view) completely inappropriate in a very human organisation where people are the inputs, people are the outputs, and people are the resources. Yet management works hard to systemise all that chaotic and wonderful humanity. At that point in this organisation lifecycle we needed leadership. Leadership to drive radical change, leadership to be strong enough to articulate vision, values and mission, leadership caring enough to express that vision and bring people onto the bus, leadership to identify where folks should sit on that bus, and leadership to create the environment where innovation and creativity could flourish.

A decade later we have grown 5 times, we have increased staff numbers and developed new products and services; we have grown from serving 600 people a year, people who experience the brutal reality of homelessness, into a young people's campus; a youth development agency with a reach into over 25,000 lives across the area.

As we have grown, at this point in our life cycle we probably need more management to help us learn how to be disciplined and focused to make sure we can repeat our astounding stuff, how can we communicate and get our messaging out to wider and wider audiences, how we understand expanding markets, how leadership ensures that it know where the organisation is on its life cycle, and how to adjust the rigging so we don't start decaying. Leadership has to be wiser, leadership has to develop systems so it knows what is working and what is not, leadership that can help us travel safely through the choppy seas, leadership that understands that storms do come, and leadership that knows how to safely sail through those storms. These recent years of austerity Britain have been a real challenge, particularly to charities.

We have been working with Roger again over the last year to help us navigate and understand the new phase of the YMCA in this rather changed market place. His book "PRIZE Winning Leadership" has become a bit of a daily reference for our team of directors. It offers simple wisdoms and sensible human truths. It helps to ground us back to reality and the real questions that need to be constantly asked: Why, What, When, Who, etc. Business can spiral into pointless complexities unless those founding principle questions are constantly applied.

So, I will use those to conclude.

Why are we engaging on a director's development strategy with Roger? Well humanly he's a great fella, he shares our values and supports our mission. I have explored the why, the reason for action, above. Roger is ultimately helping our directors grow and develop their skills and knowledge to ensure the bus keeps driving in the right direction. As we, as a team, get older, we know that sooner or later someone else will come along and begin to drive our bus.

What: we engaged Roger to lead an ongoing CPD program to build those skills, to make sure we are all sitting on the right seat of the bus. Perhaps, as CEO, I need someone else to drive the bus for a while and I need to look at the map. Roger is helping us to refocus on the map.

When: our program has already started with director's development days where Roger facilitates the discussions, brings in ideas, knowledge's and skills to encourage us to think creatively and innovate, unlocking new thoughts, affirming our gifts and talents and helping to identify and grow new ones.

Who: I guess for the foreword for this book, Roger is the **who**. I think his approach really fits our business, he shares our value base: that given the right support, training, encouragement and skills, we can change the world.

"Prize Winning Leadership" is more of a reference book for us, and it is found on my directors' desks, not on their bookshelves.

Daniel Flynn

CEO YMCA

.

Contents

ACKNOWLEDGMENTS

I want to acknowledge a huge debt of gratitude to the many marvellous minds that have contributed to my growth over the years and on whose shoulders I stand; the wisdom I have caught from many books and blogs read, videos watched, and podcasts listened to, from so many thought leaders past and present.

I would like to say a big thank you to all the friends that have shared their time with me to contribute to the journey that has produced this book. These include particularly Danny Flynn from the YMCA, Steven Roberts, Rafael Abreu and Kevin Hussey from the Life.Church Online team; Annica Törneryd and Mark Faithfull from the John Maxwell Team; Craig Walford who has been a great source of inspiration, and Sean Kennedy and Andrew Deighton who are fellow coaches.

Above all I would like to acknowledge the enthusiastic support, inspiration, and encouragement from two special people without whom my journey would have failed to get this far: Sue, my wife, I know how lucky I am to have you as my lifelong partner, I married up; and Adam, my son, of whom I am so proud, and from whom I have learned so much.

Preface

"I've always wanted to start my own business. "

Have you ever said that about anything - "I've always wanted to do ..." *this* ... or *that*. One thing that becomes very evident when you get around to doing this ... or that, is that it's so much easier to say than to do!

The opportunity to start my own business came quite unexpectedly. I had recently embarked on a new season as a sales engineer in my career with the Control Systems company where I had been a project manager for over 10 years.

"It's never too late to be what you might have been."
~ George Elliot

I had taken over this sales role from a very experienced sales engineer who was entering his retirement, and I was looking forward to my new career. Today, I was entertaining the Director of the British Nuclear Industry Forum, and just before we went out to lunch the MD asked if I could pop in to see him during the afternoon. During that afternoon meeting, I was given a life changing opportunity.

It turns out that the sector that I was selling in to was in decline, and my company had decided it no longer wanted to pursue that line of business. That meant that I had the opportunity to return to my former role as a project manager and there was quite a nice project lined up for me to take on. The alternative was to take a redundancy (severance) package if I preferred, which included a cash lump sum.

Well, I had the weekend to think about it, and that phrase "I've always wanted to ..." was a constant companion. I spent those two days with those I love and trust and explored what "might be", and the direction my life could take. We had recently moved to a new larger home (with a new mortgage) and taken on some other commitments, and so this was a challenging opportunity.

"If you plan on being anything less than you are capable of being, then you will probably be unhappy all the days of your life"
*~ **Abraham Maslow.***

Despite having no clue what I would find to do, we decided to embrace the opportunity, and I figured it this way: I would have a cash lump sum that would act as a bridge to the new career that would last a few months. If I could find some income to extend the bridge at the far end, while I consumed the bridge at the near end to pay for day to day living, then all would work out okay.

During the course of the next few months and years, I found a variety of opportunities to extend that bridge, mainly in teaching and lecturing, and also in commission based sales, that helped to make sure that the far end of the bridge kept getting further away. I discovered that "what I always wanted to do" was incredibly rewarding, incredibly challenging, and incredibly terrifying in equal measure.

"The greatest stretching seasons in life come when we do what we have never done, push ourselves harder, and reach in a way that is uncomfortable to us."
~ *John Maxwell*

I will talk about some of these challenges later in this book, however, what I wanted to share here was about the rewards that are available when we are stretched, as we embrace new opportunities and new challenges. I wanted to share some of the exhilaration of being stretched beyond what is visible and to embark on a journey that takes you into personally unchartered paths. I know that I have faced and overcome challenges that I didn't even know existed, and that I have faced and failed at things that I thought I could achieve. I also know that I wouldn't want it any other way.

"If you are no closer to your dream this year than you were last year, you can choose to accept it, defeat it, cover it up, and explain it away. Or, you can choose to change it, grow from it, and forge a new path."
~ *John Maxwell.*

I have discovered that growth doesn't happen in the Comfort Zone; I have found that the inspiration to achieve significance and the opportunity to be able to genuinely help others achieve significance is found at the far end of the bridge. I have found that there is a purpose to living and that we have the opportunity to stretch to find that purpose or choose instead to take the comfortable route.

Please hear my heart in this - I am not saying that the comfort zone is not a pleasant and enjoyable place to be, and I am not saying that we must all strive to reach our dream to achieve significance. I am not saying that everyone must stretch to risk what is, in order to reach for what might be. I am saying that for me, that journey has been immensely rewarding. I have learned to embrace these words from Rabbi Nathan, who says:

If you won't be better tomorrow than you were today,
then what do you need tomorrow for?"
~ Rabbi Nathan of Bratislav

Introduction

I've been on a journey. My journey so far includes several seasons, and I hope that I'll be here to experience and enjoy several more to come.

The last two years have brought me to a place where I wanted to share what's on my heart and write about it. The last 16 years have taken me through fascinating and unexpected places in my daily activity, in my career, in hobbies, in volunteering and in spare time activities.

"Do you know where you're going to?"
~ **sung by Diana Ross**

My life experiences have taught me to consider the theme which inspired the lyrics sung by Diana Ross that often ring through my head from the film 'Mahogany': "Do you know where you're going to?". The theme of this song is based on evaluating life's journey so far, and asking if what lies ahead is what you really want. I guess it's my musical inclination along with the era I grew up in that makes this song and these lyrics resonate so well with me when I think of leadership.

I think I could probably find a tune that reflects my experiences and thinking for most seasons of my life and career, and this one, in particular, brings a haunting yet exciting and challenging tone. For me, one thing that comes out of it is the idea that we're all on a journey, from here to there. Here and there are different places for each one of us, and they can be different places during each season of life, but we all have somewhere for each place for each season we're in.

Leadership can also be described as taking people with us from here to there. If there is no 'there' to go to why do we need a leader. If there is no-one following the leader then, as John Maxwell says, she is simply taking a walk.

This book is divided into three sections entitled DREAM, DELIVER and DEVELOP. These reflect the leadership journey of firstly figuring out where "there" is, then the journey of getting there, and finally a season to reflect and grow, to find where the next there is.

> *"Your PRIZE is the reason you get up in the morning, and often the last thing you think about as you fall asleep at night."*

The central theme in PRIZE winning leadership is that "there" needs to be Inspirational for you. If it's inspirational, it will have something that makes us want to get up in the morning and take the next step, even on "those days" when life seems to conspire against us; it will have something that is frequently the last thing we think about as we fall asleep at night.

A key ingredient in this process is to be on the lookout for something NEW, your Next Exciting Win. These are stepping stones between where you are now and where you want to be next, and form a series of exciting steps along the way.

> *"The decisions you make today will determine the stories you tell tomorrow."*
> ~ **Craig Groeschel**

Each chapter in the book addresses a part of this journey and adds a piece in the jigsaw of life to help get there. Part ONE (Dream) looks first at the PRIZE, where to find the Inspiration Zone and your Next Exciting Win. It explores your Dream and how to Imagine it, to find it, and to define it.

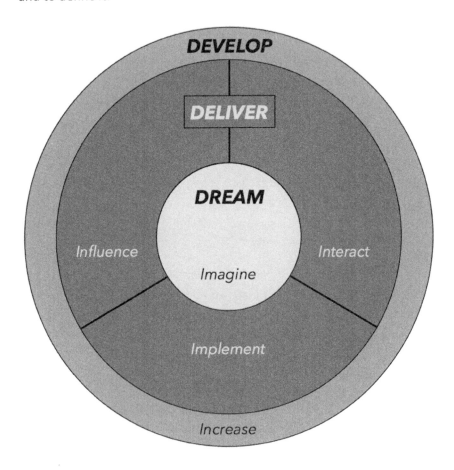

Part TWO (Deliver) looks at Influence, Interaction and Implementation. It has been said that "Leadership is Influence" and I know that short statement can't possibly hold all the answers, but it reveals a key core element. Without influence, a leader won't be able to lead anyone anywhere and we explore this in chapter 3. So many people try to communicate yet fail to connect with those around them, and chapter 4 looks at this, while chapter 5 explores the 6S Implementation

Framework that has developed from over 15 years of project management experience.

Part THREE (Develop) is all about Increase and personal growth, and Chapter 6 has several stories from my experience. It finishes by coming back to reflect on where I started out in the preface and encourages us not to miss the collateral beauty of life's experiences. Experiences can have hard lessons to teach us, but there is often a beauty that emerges from the ashes that could so easily be missed.

Each chapter has a concluding question that asks: "So What!". It is in asking ourselves this question and digging in to find the answer, that we will take lasting benefit from reading this, and any similar book. I encourage you to pause and reflect and to write down your answers to these questions before moving on from one chapter to the next. I would also love to hear from you as you walk with me through this book, and hear the "So What" moments that come your way.

"The most glorious moments in your life are not the so-called days of success, but rather those days when out of dejection and despair you feel rise in you a challenge to life, and the promise of future accomplishments."
*~ **Gustave Flaubert***

Do you know where you're going to?

Do you know where you're going to?
Do you like the things
that life is showing you?
Where are you going to?
Do you know?

Do you get what you're hoping for?
When you look behind you
There's no open door
What are you hoping for?
Do you know?

Once we were standing still in time
Chasing the fantasies that filled our minds
You knew I loved you
But my spirit was free
Laughing at the questions
That you once ask me

Now, looking back at all we've planned
We've let so many dreams
Just slip through our hands
Why must we wait so long before we'll see
How sad the answers to those questions can be?

"Do you know where you're going to?" was written by Michael Masser and
Gerald Goffin and sung by Diana Ross in the film Mahogany.
It was initially recorded by American singer Thelma Houston in 1973,
and more recently by Mariah Carey.

PART ONE

DREAM

If leadership is taking people on a journey from here to there ...

Where is there?

Do you know where you're going to?
Do you like the things that life is showing you?

Chapter 1

PRIZE Winning Leadership

"Cadets, listen up and pay attention to your Commanding Officer. Next month we have a few opportunities for cadets to participate in the Glider Flying program. All cadets interested in applying, one pace forward; March."

I was there when I was 14.

Have you ever had a dream of doing something really exciting? Maybe it was an exotic holiday, or perhaps it was learning an instrument, or maybe a great new business idea.

I was a cadet in an organisation called the "Air Training Corps" - that's the Royal Air Force (RAF) for young people. I can't remember why I joined initially, but I rather suspect it was my dad's idea since I was somewhat rebellious as a teenager.

Anyway, from time to time we had the opportunity to go on trips to do fun things. I remember one day when the CO asked us *"Would any of you cadets like to have the opportunity to join the Glider Flying Program."*

I volunteered like a shot! I had always loved the idea of flying and I loved learning everything about it.

As I recall I was scared witless before we took off and we were airborne for less than 10 minutes, but I absolutely loved it. During that time, I can remember the absolute elation of flying, of experiencing the miracle of flight personally, of just hanging there in mid-air, of the magnificent views; you could see for miles. That feeling never left me.

Some years later I was chatting with my friend John in our local pub. John runs the local branch of a national charity and he is always on the lookout for some fun fundraising activities. So, when John said to me: *"I've been thinking about this year's fundraising, and what about if we get a few of us together to do a parachute jump. We should be able to raise some funds doing that and have some fun doing it too."*

I immediately recalled the elation I had experienced when flying the glider, so when John came up with this idea I was full of bravado and said: *"That's a great idea, I'm up for that; I've always wanted to do a parachute jump!"*

Well, it turns out that they do static line jumps at Langar Airfield in Nottingham which isn't far from where we live, and five of us signed up to do a jump to raise some money for the charity. I remember the journey to the Airfield, and if you'd been sitting in John's blue SUV with us you would have heard loads of witty banter and bravado and we all sounded pretty confident. As we arrived at the airfield and turned the corner into the entrance the car suddenly fell very silent, as we spotted the plane that we were going to jump out of that weekend.

We spent an entire day learning about all the things that could possibly go wrong with jumping out of a plane. The instructor explained: *"Sometimes when you jump out, part of the parachute mechanism can get caught on the wing or some other part of the plane, then I'll have to climb down to you and then cut us both free! If your lines get twisted, which sometimes happens, then you'll need to learn how to kick out with your legs so that you can untwist the lines."*

I remember glancing across at John and saw that he looked just as worried as I felt! We spent a good while learning what to do if the main parachute didn't deploy and how to release the emergency chute, and we practiced how to land at speed without breaking anything.

Having spent all day learning about everything that could go wrong with jumping out of a plane we went home, to return the next day to give it a go, weather permitting. I remember looking up and it was a fairly chilly and overcast day but apparently, the cloud cover was high enough for us to do our jump.

During the morning, we sat together on a bench near the landing area and had the opportunity to watch some of the regular members do all sorts of aerobatics on the way down. We patiently waited until our turn finally came along, and off we went to collect our parachutes and strap them on.

We made our way out to the plane and having figured out who sat where, I made sure to line up so that I would be the first one out of the plane, and we took off with the instructor straddling the empty doorway so we couldn't fall out as we took off.

After we had reached the correct height and we approached the drop zone the instructor gestured across to me to indicate that I should edge towards the doorway, and I sat as I had been instructed, one cheek on the plane and one in mid-air, gripping the doorway, and then I saw the instructor shout: *"JUMP"* and I leapt out of the plane spreading out my arms and legs, arched my back and looked upwards to see the parachute unfurling.

I soon realised that my lines were actually twisted and the parachute wasn't going to deploy properly. After an initial mind freeze and thoughts of "oh ... dear" (or *something* like that) I almost instinctively did the "kick out" thing that I had been taught earlier to untwist the lines, and the parachute deployed and there I was, suspended in mid-air, flying solo, with an absolutely magnificent view for miles around. All I could hear was the wind in my ears and it felt like I was flying. I spent the next few minutes having fun steering the chute around in circles first this way then that way and really experienced that elation again, before having to aim for the landing spot. Finally, I landed, and the exhilaration I felt having actually done a jump on my own was unbelievable!

Now maybe you're not that bothered about jumping out of a perfectly good aeroplane that's going to land soon anyway. So here's a question for you: what's that thing that you've always wanted to do? Maybe it's something like learning a new language so you can order a drink when you're on holiday? Maybe it's learning a new sport so that you can enjoy getting fitter and shed some excess weight? Maybe you've got a really great product idea and you just haven't got around to doing anything about it or a book you need to write.

I remember having this great idea when websites were a new thing and every company was getting one, and that was to have a site where everyone would go to browse through all of the houses for sale in an area without having to visit each company's site in turn. I did nothing about that idea.

So, what could this look like for me?

- The first step is to **Recognise your Dream**.
- Then you need to **Respond to your Challenges**.
- Finally, you need to **Realise your Ambitions**

I'll be unpacking these ideas in more detail in the following chapters, but for now here's the "tops of the waves" of what this could look like.

Recognise your Dream

More than likely your dream will be linked to your **Sweet-Spot**. (See more about the sweet-spot in chapter 2.) Everyone has one - just as a cricket bat has one, and a golf club does too, and a tennis racket ... when you find the sweet-spot it just feels so good! Your sweet-spot is the place where your experiences, resources and values overlap to bring excitement and reward.

For me, growing up, my dream was to fly. Later on, it involved learning to speak French sufficiently well that I could move up the corporate ladder in a French company. More recently in 2002, it had to do with setting out on my own and launching my consultancy business, and serving on the board of directors for several others. For Sue, my wife it often has something to do with getting the extended family together, and recently we all went on a weekend away together.

Respond to your Challenges

For this we need to understand what happens outside of our comfort zone, and how to get there safely. Outside of the comfort zone there is a place I've called the **Inspiration Zone** (we'll explore that more in just a minute), and that's located just beyond what I'll call the Fear Barrier. This means that to find the Inspiration Zone you need to step outside of your comfort zone and step across the fear barrier.

For me, to pursue my dream of flying, that flight in the glider and the Parachute Jump were definitely right there, beyond the fear barrier. Learning a foreign language was certainly there, as I had failed my French O'Level quite spectacularly, twice.

So if your dream is to be a public speaker, maybe the challenge of signing up to deliver your first talk is just beyond the fear barrier. Perhaps your dream is to write a book and your challenge is to write the first chapter or the outline, or if you want to get fitter, maybe your challenge is doing a 10k run.

Realise your Ambitions

For this, you need to do something *NEW*. That's your **Next Exciting Win**. Your **N**ext **E**xciting **W**in is like a stepping stone towards your dream; something challenging and exciting that you can commit to, and that takes you towards your dream.

The Eagle and the Hawk
I am the eagle, I live in high country,
In rocky cathedrals that reach to the sky,
I am the hawk and there's blood on my feathers,
But time is still turning, they soon will be dry,
And all those who see me, and all who believe in me,
Share in the freedom I feel when I fly!
~ John Denver

The Inspiration Zone

To discover how to find the Inspiration Zone we first need to explore the comfort zone. I visit my comfort zone when I am doing something I am familiar with and that I enjoy doing. I love to play bass guitar in my local band; I love to play my violin, either in my local orchestra or as a soloist, and I love to travel and visit family.

For these to actually be in my comfort zone I need to know the music and I need to have practised of course and to travel I need to have the tickets ready and the route all planned out.

For me, when I need to learn a new piece of music, or travel to a new destination then I need to step outside of my comfort zone a little and there are all sorts of challenges to be found there. For me it conjures up an image of a soldier in enemy territory returning to base after a short reconnaissance mission and saying "... it's a jungle out there Captain", and I am reminded of the theme tune to the TV series "Monk":

It's a jungle out there
Disorder and confusion everywhere
No one seems to care ...
... You better pay attention
Or this world we love so much might just kill you
~ Randy Newman

There are some things and places that are outside my comfort zone that I'll never want to visit because I'm just not interested, or I don't have the skill or ability. For me this currently includes things like finding a "nice new recipe" to cook, participating in a reality TV show or climbing a mountain. I've no interest in those activities at all, and I'm no good at any of them either.

However, there are some things that I might be interested in pursuing that are outside my comfort zone. I like to call this place outside of my comfort zone the "discomfort zone", and to get there I need to step over the fear barrier.

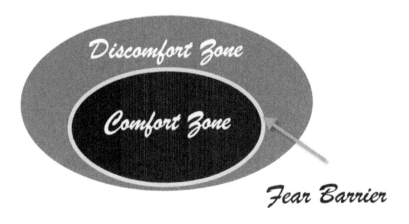

The fear barrier is something that causes us to take a sharp intake of breath; it's the "oh dear" moment when I realise that I will have to do "that" thing to get there, such as jumping out of a plane on my own at 3,000 feet to find my lines are tangled! There are some places in this discomfort zone that I'm never likely to visit because of that particular fear. For example, as much as I enjoy exercise and I have enjoyed participating in some cycle races in the past I'll never enter the Tour de France (or the Tour of Britain, or the tour of anywhere for that matter); I enjoy playing the violin and bass guitar but I'll never enter a TV talent show or I'm unlikely to play in a professional band.

At this point we need to understand why we want to go there anyway. What is it that draws us to step outside of our comfort zone? This is when we come across the Inspiration Zone. This is somewhere I visit when I am inspired to want to step outside my comfort zone.

There is something Inspirational about the place I want to visit that enables me to cross over the fear barrier, to deal with the fear so that I can achieve that inspirational dream or goal. I wrote earlier that for me the dream of flying inspired me to take a flight in a glider as a cadet and do a parachute jump some years later. In my career I wanted to become a Project Manager, and there were many challenges I had to negotiate and overcome before that dream became a reality.

I learned an important principle of following a dream: Is my dream inspirational, does it continue to inspire me? In order to remain a compelling dream, it needs to stay in the Inspiration Zone.

Many of us spend a lot of our time in our comfort zone. That's the place where we feel at home. We find our strengths there, and we find the things we enjoy doing there.

The Inspiration Zone is found outside there in the discomfort zone, beyond the fear barrier, but it has something about it that is inspirational. To learn and memorise a new tune means I get to play it onstage without faults. The inspiration comes both from not making mistakes onstage, and from expanding my repertoire of the music that I enjoy playing. To do a parachute jump means jumping out of a plane at 3,000 feet and conquering a fear of heights, and enjoying the thrill of flying.

The bigger the dream, the bigger the inspiration needed to help us get through the fear barrier to achieve it. However there is another end to the Inspiration Zone.

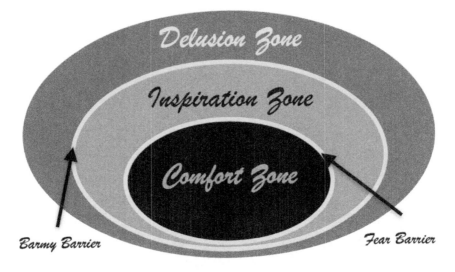

With insufficient inspiration then the fear barrier wins, and we back off from achieving that dream. With too much enthusiasm and insufficient ability then we are at risk of finding the Delusion Zone, a place that is usually reserved for those frequently shown in the first few rounds of X-Factor, those who have a dream that is not backed up by the ability to deliver the dream.

Beware the Barmy Barrier, and make sure that your dream is in reach.

Personally Rewarding Inspiration Zone Experience

It's all about the bass! Well, for me it is for sure. One of the things in my "bucket list" included playing bass regularly, better still to play a *5-string* bass regularly, and even better - occasionally a 5-string *fretless* bass (a bass guitar with a smooth fingerboard, like double basses)!

Because you know I'm all about that bass,
'Bout that bass, no treble
I'm all 'bout that bass, 'bout that bass, no treble
I'm all 'bout that bass, 'bout that bass, no treble
I'm all 'bout that bass, 'bout that bass
*~ **Songwriters: Kevin Kadish / Meghan Trainor***

I love music, and I love playing music. I've been playing an instrument for as long as I can remember, from starting piano lessons at 5 and then violin at 8, and turning my hand to playing keyboard, strumming an acoustic guitar and playing the harmonica along the way too.

So when a friend of mine asked if I would like to play bass in their band I immediately jumped at the chance! I had a cheap bass guitar and an old combo amp, and I had even played a few gigs more than 10 years previously, so I immediately embraced the opportunity. I hadn't been playing anything regularly for a while so I was quite excited at the prospect of playing again.

"To succeed in life we must stay within our strength zone, but continually move outside our comfort zone."
~John Maxwell

It wasn't until after I had obtained a copy of the music that we would be playing and started to practice that I remembered: we don't use music on stage. Not only would I have to learn the pieces, I would have to remember them to be able to play them on stage without music!

Now, some people seem to be blessed with a good memory and can recall names and faces, song lyrics and place names with ease. I am not one of those people. In fact, I would put it this way:

"I have a great forgettory. If you want something forgetting, let me know and I'll forget it for you."

My passion for music and my eagerness to play bass led me to confront my self-doubt and to start working diligently to learn the pieces, and to memorise them to be able to perform on stage. On one of my early outings, a member of the audience asked the sound crew to turn the bass up because they couldn't hear it, only to discover that "the bassist isn't playing" because I was struggling to remember the notes. However, I persevered and found ways to help me remember my part, and I now play regularly throughout the year!

"If you are working on something exciting that you really care about, you don't have to be pushed. The vision pulls you."
~ Steve Jobs

So how do you discover what your passion is? Well, your passion, your dream, usually has a PRIZE. That's a **Personally Rewarding, Inspiration Zone Experience**. The Inspiration Zone is never found inside of your comfort zone, and you have to go beyond the place where you are comfortable in order to find Inspiration to pursue a meaningful PRIZE.

"If I were to wish for anything, I should not wish for wealth and power, but for the passionate sense of the potential, for the eye which, ever young and ardent, sees the possible. Pleasure disappoints, possibility never. And what wine is so sparkling, what so fragrant, what so intoxicating, as possibility!"
~ Søren Kierkegaard

Think about the prizes you have won, think about the reward obtained from winning each prize. For me, my prizes have included flying, learning to speak French fluently, getting married, starting my own business, playing bass guitar on stage, and writing my first book. If you don't yet know what your prize is or where to find it, then we'll be discussing that more in the next Chapter.

Then think what you had to do to achieve your prize, and you'll see that the more rewarding prizes are found further outside of the Comfort Zone. What's more, the further outside your comfort zone the prize is found, the greater the inspiration required to pursue it.

Oh, and I have now upgraded to a 5-string Overwater and a 5-string fretless Ibanez that I play regularly.

The Dip

I had started my new passion of playing my 5-string Overwater bass guitar in my new band; I absolutely loved it. I loved every minute of playing and practicing and having the opportunity to play in the band with some great musicians.

I was eagerly learning new material every week, as I practiced the songs to catch up with the rest of the band who had all been playing together for some time. As each week passed I discovered new ways of improving my practice time. There are still techniques that I will need time to focus practice on to even start to play, and there are others where I can see some really encouraging progress and I start to be able to play something that I had previously struggled with.

"If you are not growing and developing yourself in the pursuit of your dream, it may be time to identify a new one. Your journey must be fulfilling.
~ John Maxwell

I learned another feature of following dreams too. Not only does it need to stay in the Inspiration Zone, it will often encounter what Seth Godin calls a *Dip* in his book by the same name.

"The decision to quit or not is a simple evaluation: Is the pain of the Dip worth the benefit of the light at the end of the tunnel?"

"Quitting is better than coping because quitting frees you up to excel at something else. At the beginning, when you first start something, it's fun. Over the next few days and weeks, the rapid learning you experience keeps you going. Whatever your new thing is, it's easy to stay engaged in it. And then the Dip happens. The Dip is the long slog between starting and mastery. A long slog that's actually a shortcut, because it gets you where you want to go faster than any other path."
~ Seth Godin

For me playing bass the dips were usually found in a new song that had a quite impossible bass line. How anyone could play it at all was a total mystery. However, with some dedicated listening to figure out what was being played I started to master each of these songs in turn. Some needed a few prompts on the practice sheet to remind me of the rhythm, while others needed to be transcribed in full so that I could practice slowly at first and then gradually speed up. Curiously the songs that were initially the hardest to learn, became the most entrenched in my memory and easiest to remember by the time I had mastered them!

"The journey is better than the inn"
~ Miguel de Cervantes

It turns out that in the achievement of a dream it is often the journey that has produced the most important outcome in what or who you become in the process. *"Is going through the Dip worth the benefit of the light at the end of the tunnel?"* In hindsight, it is sometimes going through the Dip that has produced the most significant, meaningful and useful learning and long lasting growth.

Sitting in a training course in France with only French being spoken and getting to the end of a day exhausted and having to spend hours every night trying to catch up, that's a dip.

Launching a company and working through the days and weeks when no business seems to be coming in to cover the costs, that's a dip.

Spending many days tendering for work and finishing second, time after time, that's a dip.

One thing's for sure, we'll not be the first person to encounter it, and we'll not be the last!

When we're in the middle of the dip, and everything feels like the PRIZE is out of reach, how would you feel or what would you think about if you supposed for a moment that it's not?

The Dip is the long slog between starting and mastery. A long slog that's actually a shortcut, because it gets you where you want to go faster than any other path."
~ Seth Godin

Next Exciting Win

When I heard the song we were going to learn next and listened to the bass line, my jaw dropped and I listened in admiration, and then I remembered, "*I am going to have to try to play that!*"

This particular piece had so many elements I would have to master; syncopated rhythms, very intricate fast-moving passages, and slap bass! "*Where do I even start!*" (Slap bass is an impressive advanced technique of playing that I have yet to fully master). I discovered that the secret is found in the words of H. Jackson Brown:

"Two rules of perseverance:
Rule #1 Take one more step.
Rule #2 When you can't take one more step, refer to Rule #1"
~ H. Jackson Brown

I had been working through some online lessons using the website from the awesome bass guru Scott Devine at *ScottsBassLessons.com* and this new song brought renewed determination to master at least some of these new elements of playing to do justice to the original.

To make this come alive I had to make out a path of progression, and I drew inspiration from each successful step along the path towards a credible performance. I discovered that the most effective route was to make each step exciting along the way. I haven't yet completely mastered the bass line of the song, but I am getting better every time we play it!

To reach for your reward you have to do something **NEW** - that's your **N**ext **E**xciting **W**in. The Next Exciting Win is a challenge, a stepping stone if you like, that takes me towards my **PRIZE** (my *Personally Rewarding, Inspiration Zone Experience*).

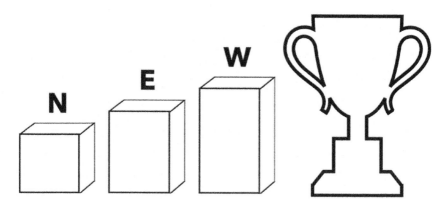

So to learn the new piece I had to find ways to make a progression through a series of **NEW** tasks that brought excitement and reward with each step. For me, the first step was to understand what was being played. I worked on figuring out the chords and the rhythm of the main verse and chorus and then attempted to replicate that. My wife Sue was my delighted audience, having to sit through a spirited performance of each successive improvement.

All great masters are chiefly distinguished by the power of adding a second, a third, and perhaps a fourth step in a continuous line. Many a man had taken the first step. With every additional step, you enhance immensely the value of you first.
~ Ralph Waldo Emerson

Having started to master the main elements of the piece the next was to attempt to learn the fast parts and the slap technique. For this, I enlisted the help of a friend called Raul who is an awesome bassist. I met up with Raul on a vacation trip, and when we met I discovered that he had released a video tutorial of that very bass part, so I added that to my library to work on when I returned from vacation.

The mastery of these two elements still eludes me but I have managed to substitute something that works well in their place for now, and I look forward to mastering the part completely one day.

The key to success is to keep doing something **NEW.**

The key is to try to make each step exciting and to celebrate the win. It's when each step becomes a drudge that progress becomes dreary and motivation wanes. The key to success is to keep doing something **NEW**.

"Everyone faces difficulty when working towards a dream. And if someone fails he can make excuses for what went wrong, how the unexpected happened, how someone let him down, how circumstances worked against him. But the reality is that the external things do not stop people. It's what happens to them on the inside."
~ John Maxwell

So What!

So what three things stood out to you most in this chapter?

So what is the first thing you want to share with someone else?

So what is one thing you plan to do differently?

So what NEW thing could you achieve in the next six weeks?

Chapter 2

Imagine

I was once talking with a vicar about a recent funeral that he had conducted of a wealthy local resident, and he said he had been asked how much the deceased had left. He leant over to me to share his answer, lowered his voice to a conspiratorial whisper and said: "Everything".

Stephen Covey talks about leaving a legacy as the highest of four human dimensions, occupying the same place as self-actualisation in Maslow's well-known hierarchy of needs. Tony Robbins has described this as the two "Needs of the spirit" for Growth and Contribution, and others too have explored this space.

"To live, to love, and to leave a legacy."
~ Stephen Covey

It has been said that we will all have a *life sentence*, a sentence that is used to describe our lives after we are long gone. If we can get the chance to influence what that sentence will be during our lifetime, what would we like it to say? If we want to create an intentional legacy then it may be worth considering before it has become history.

In order to explore what our legacy might be the most popular and effective approach is to seek what is usually called your **"sweet-spot"**. In sports such as cricket or baseball that refers to the part of the bat which yields the best connection with the ball and with the right stroke sends the ball out of the park. So far as personal development is concerned it has a similar meaning, of finding what makes you and me unique and using that uniqueness to best effect.

Jim Collins in his book *"Good to Great"* discusses the following three questions, and questions similar to these can be found in various places elsewhere:

What can you be the best in the world at?
What drives your economic engine?
What are you deeply passionate about?

Many people struggle with achieving adequate clarity with these three questions and might say "I don't think I can be world class at anything", "I'm not really passionate about anything", or "I care about so many things I can't choose.

"Everyone ends up somewhere, but few people end up somewhere on purpose"
~ *Craig Groeschel*

A key element that these questions all seem to miss is: "What is life telling you?" A really helpful way to explore that is to consider your past experiences and to do that in such a way that you can draw the lessons from them. This is especially helpful for those people that feel less than certain in finding a solution from the previous three questions and often acts as a reinforcement of the conclusions for those that did find an answer.

For me, a key phrase that emerged from that exercise was that "everything I've done, I've taught". I discovered that my passion is "helping people learn", and I'll explore that a little more in the next section. It's also true that there have been several times in my life when I have felt quite directionless and that nothing seemed to rise up passionately in me at all. Sometimes those are periods where other pressures are dictating where life leads, and sometimes they are periods where a new direction is needed to bring a spark back into every day living.

Craig Groeschel has produced several resources that can be used to help with this journey and they are all available for free from a website dedicated to the subject. This can be found at a site that uses the Hebrew word for "Dream" or "Vision" in the title, at www.chazown.com, from which the SERVE Program is derived.

"Your past often holds the key to unlock your future"
*~ **Craig Groeschel***

Here, along with exploring our core values and our natural gifts, we are encouraged to draw out a timeline from our experiences, and pay particular attention to the key experiences that were maybe painful or difficult to experience, and to draw out the main lessons that emerge from that analysis. It is often through exploring both our sorrows and our successes that we become prepared to fulfil our purpose and to leave a uniquely personal legacy.

What people say, what people do, and what they say they do are entirely different things.
~Margaret Mead

People say a lot, and they do a lot; to know what they believe watch what they do. By exploring our past in terms of what we've done, by exploring both the sorrows and successes and drawing the threads that connect them together we can gather a valuable insight into ourselves, our values, our passions and our strengths. This can then bring some additional clarity into the three questions that we explored earlier from Jim Collins and can help us to understand the legacy that we want to leave as our life sentence.

SERVE Program

'Let me reflect on that, and I'll let you know.' Anyone in sales knows that usually means "no". However, when it comes to personal growth, it usually means "there is a lesson in there somewhere, and I need to try and find it".

I had a significant "Aha!" moment recently that came out of the blue when I wasn't expecting it. It was while I was reflecting on the outcome from attending a course designed to discover the purpose for your life, and boy has it had a significant effect on the direction of my life.

"Experience isn't the best teacher; evaluated experience is."
~ John Maxwell.

Way back in Roman times, in an account written on the Civil War (Commentarii de Bello Civili), Julius Caesar is credited with saying that *'Experience is the teacher of all things'*, however Water Scott (1854-1900) disagrees with the proverb, saying that *'experience is the name everyone gives to their mistakes.'* I suspect that there is wisdom in both sayings, and perhaps the best summary is summed up by Maxwell as: *"Experience isn't the best teacher; evaluated experience is."*

"Follow effective action with quiet reflection. From the quiet reflection will come even more effective action."
~ Peter Drucker

I had signed up to attend an event which I had wanted to get along to for a while, despite having done the "Sweet-spot" exercise several times over the years. What is the sweet-spot exercise? Well it's usually designed to help a person find their place and purpose in life's journey by evaluating three or four headings and finding where they intersect or overlap.

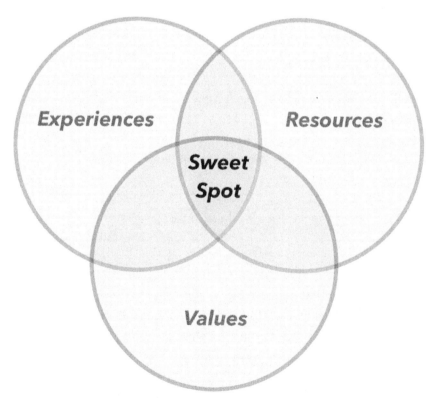

This particular program encourages the participants to evaluate themselves using the three headings or prompts of Personal Experiences, Personal Resources, and Personal Values. The one that is fairly unusual in my experience is to include personal experiences in quite the way this program uses. For me this is where the dawning of a new direction emerged.

Looking back over my timeline during that event started me on a personal journey of reflection that I guess brought into the light some key thoughts that had been present all along, but just sitting quietly in the shadows. The key thought that emerged from this exercise is that right from the earliest times it would be true to say that in many cases "*everything I have done, I have taught*", and that applies to sport and music, as well as more academic topics. That was the first of three key thoughts that emerged.

In a teaching, training or coaching environment I have often been heard to ask students "*what are you here for*", to which they usually reply, "*to learn*". "*And what am I here for?*" ... "*to teach*". My reply to that is usually "*If I am only here to teach, then I can teach and even if you go away having learned nothing I have done my job. No, I am here 'to help you learn'; if you go away having learned nothing then I have NOT done my job!*" That brought the next key thought into the light.

"I'm not here to teach, I'm here to help you learn."

The third key thought that emerged from that evaluation of my experiences, and that kept emerging was that my passion and gift is in the field of leadership, and that had been manifest in coming alongside several leaders and teams, and helping them to become better at leading the mission they were engaged in. A colleague recently commented:

"Rarely is someone's vocation and anointing shown to me so clearly as yours. Roger's approach and insight into leadership and management understanding is both profound and contextually vibrant."
~ Craig Walford

Here started a journey that brought me to the visit I made the following year to a certification event that marked a turning point in my career.

The event I attended then is now available as a **SERVE** Program. This program is based on finding your **S**weet-spot, by exploring your Personal **E**xperiences, your Personal **R**esources (strengths and abilities), and your Personal **V**alues, and where they all come together to generate **E**xcitement, and reward.

SERVE. *Find your*
Sweet-spot, *by exploring your Personal*
*- **Experiences,** your Personal*
*- **Resources** (strengths and abilities), and your Personal*
*- **Values.** They all combine to generate Personal*
Excitement *and reward.*

In the light of attending the SERVE program I embarked on a leadership certification program, which led to becoming certified as an independent Speaker, Coach and Trainer with a world class Leadership Expert and his team.

Early on in my career I spent several hours in airports on business journeys around Europe, and much of my waiting time was spent browsing the contents of the airport bookshops, which inevitably had several business-related books on offer. Titles from Peter Drucker and Ken Blanchard were a regular favourite.

I first came into contact with the work of John C Maxwell in the late '90s, and had enjoyed several titles on the topic of leadership, and got to know his work in more detail during a three-year program called "The Million Leaders Mandate" in the 2000s which I attended with a colleague. More recently in 2014, John Maxwell was listed as the No. 1 leader in business by the American Management Association, and the most influential leadership expert in the world by Business Insider and Inc. Magazine, and he leads the field according to Global Gurus and many other observers. What better place to obtain my Speaking, Coaching and Training certification. Since the quote below he has now sold over 26 million books in fifty languages.

"John C. Maxwell is an internationally recognized as the best leadership speaker, trainer and author who has written over 70 books and sold more than 19 million copies."
~ Global Gurus

Looking back on the SERVE Program, it will come as no surprise to those that know me that having signed up to attend, I ended up leading one of the break out groups to facilitate discussion, and delivering the talk to lead one of the key sessions.

What's your dream?

Apparently, nine out of ten adults have or want a pursuit that ignites their passionate side. That's what the study conducted by Alpha Romeo found as part of their recent #FindYourPassion campaign.

The campaign was designed by the iconic car company to illustrate the passion that Alpha Romeo brings to their corporate ethos, and to help the British public put passion back into their lives. Over half of those responding (57%) listed Sir David Attenborough as the most passionate person in the UK.

> "Without passion you may run out of steam before you reach your dream."
> ~ **John Maxwell**

After the veteran broadcaster, naturalist and environmental campaigner, the Harry Potter author JK Rowling was second, then the increasingly popular physicist who brings science to the masses, Professor Brian Cox, along with the leader of the Scottish National Party Nicola Sturgeon, were both close behind.

This research also found that nearly half of the respondents (46%) confirmed that they don't have the time to pursue a passion due to pressures of work, while those who did have something they were passionate about indicated that they were happier and healthier than those without such a passion.

Over the last 18 months or so I have been working with an organisation who have an international team of over 600 comprising mainly volunteers from some 40 countries; it's fascinating to work with a team that is so connected to a core mission and that are passionate about what they do.

One of the hallmarks of this team is that the volunteers are all so obviously passionate about their work, and spend many dedicated hours every week to ensure that the mission and purpose are carried out with enthusiasm. It's really inspiring to see such dedication from such a large multinational team.

> *A key question to ask about any dream, vision or mission statement is the passion question: "Does my dream compel me to follow it?"*

So what are the hallmarks of a dream that make it consistently important for those pursuing that dream to continue pursuing it with enthusiasm for years on end? Well, here are four things that can help provide energy for a dream:

Take into account your natural temperament

We're not all the same. Obvious, I know, and probably a very good thing! However, it is important to understand your natural temperament when exploring your dream and make sure that the part you play draws on your natural strengths and temperament so that you stay committed in the long run. Is this dream really MY dream?

Keep an eye on what's important to you

It is important to remember what drew you to the dream in the first place, and to keep the main thing, the main thing. It can be too easy to get distracted by the day to day pressures and lose sight of what you were drawn to in the first place. Too many people start to pursue a passion for one reason and then lose that passion for another reason entirely. Do I have the energy to pursue it?

Overcome the fear of being different from others

You can't be part of the crowd and achieve your dream at the same time. If you have been following a dream passionately it is inevitable that you'll stand out from those that aren't, and it's okay to be different. Am I willing to pay the price?

Resist the apathy that often comes with time

I have been involved in selling control system projects for many years, and there is a well-known challenge that causes companies to make a great start and then to begin losing customers. The first project is costed up based on the best estimate of the work involved and the likely challenges. A subsequent project has the benefit of understanding some of the unforeseen pitfalls and problems, and that can cause the cost estimates to be gradually increased until there are so many contingencies built in that the project is overpriced and the business is lost. In the same way, an apathy can settle in over some time to the routine of pursuing a passion when focus shifts from the payoff to the problems encountered along the way. How do I keep the main thing, the main thing?

One definition of Passion is: "It's the thing you are thinking about when you should be thinking about something else!"

So what's that thing you're thinking about now? It probably isn't anything to do with the environment, or with the science of the cosmos, or even getting involved with an international volunteer activity, but what do you think about when you should be thinking about something else, and what are you going to do about it?

Uncomfortable comfort

I knew that I was hopeless at languages. After all, at school, I had been advised not to take a course in German, and I had failed my French O'Level quite spectacularly, twice.

Later, while working for a French company, I ended up spending some months on a placement in France, and when I arrived back in England I discovered to my amazement that I was now placed in the "advanced" language class!

Unless you try to do something beyond what you have already mastered, you will never grow."
~ Ralf Waldo Emerson

What I learned from that experience was that from school days I had developed a belief that "I was hopeless at languages". It had been instilled in me by teachers and reinforced by results. But, that belief wasn't serving me well, and it was actually responsible for holding me back from moving forward in my career.

To illustrate this point, let me give you another example. As a teenager, I had been really fit and active, playing many different sports from rugby to cycling to hammer throwing, and I loved the activity and team dynamics. Hardly a day went by when I wasn't doing one activity or another, and I even managed to obtain some paid work as a skating instructor for a few years.

Then after I graduated and started work, got married and started a family, I seemed to find less and less time to be involved in any kind of sports, and when I did have the time it wasn't sufficiently often to allow me to participate in any kind of team game that needed regular attendance. So my health habits declined until I found myself carrying quite a lot of extra weight. I decided that maybe since I was past my 20s and into my 30s now I should just accept this new version of me.

"Move out of your comfort zone. You can only grow if you are willing to feel awkward and uncomfortable when you try something new."
~ Brian Tracey

One day, however, after catching sight of my quite portly figure in some summer holiday photos I decided it was about time to do something about it. I contacted a friend of mine who I knew had managed to lose over 11 stone in weight (that's over 150 lbs for our American friends), slimming down from 26 to 15 stone. in just over a year. It turned out that he had joined a slimming club and that had given him the support he needed to start and persevere with a slimming program. Well, I found that I believed that if it worked for him it could work for me, so I joined my local club and started getting along once a week after work.

For me though, and maybe it was just the group I was attending, I didn't really enjoy or look forward to the group meetings after the first few, and although this had got me started it wasn't going to get me to my target. It had helped me to start a change in mind-set, to get started on the journey, and I had lost quite a lot of weight in a few weeks, but I didn't yet fully believe I could achieve the results I was after.

"Find your comfort zone. Then leave it."
~ Robert Kiosaki

After a few weeks I decided to join a local gym instead of attending the slimming club, and before long I was enjoying getting along for a short workout every lunchtime during the week. I was now seeing some really great results both in fitness and weight loss and I was feeling so much better in myself, and now I was starting to believe that I could achieve the target I needed to reach to regain a healthy level of fitness and weight.

It was the next step that really made all the difference though. That was when I decided to start cycling to work every day, and before long I had settled into a routine for my commute that became a daily habit. Initially, the route to work was just 10 miles each way, and then after moving to a new house it had extended to over 15 miles each way, and most days I used a route that was some 20 miles each way, and much longer on sunny summer evenings.

"The sooner you step away from your comfort zone you'll realise that it really wasn't that comfortable."
~ Eddie Harris Jr.

I had changed my belief that I would have to accept the overweight version of myself and now had a new belief that I could once again be fit and healthy. You see, like habits, our beliefs are stored in our subconscious mind. This means that by definition they are below the level of our consciousness. That means that we are not necessarily aware of what we believe until we (or a good coach) question our beliefs, and we are able to change our beliefs to support a new reality.

"Get comfortable being uncomfortable. Get confident being uncertain. Don't give up just because something is hard. Pushing through challenges is what makes you grow."
~ Jules Marcoux

I'm getting married in the morning

When Sue and I got married some 30+ years ago, we decided to spend our honeymoon in Italy on the Amalfi Coast. It was a stunning location with a lovely hotel and a fabulous area to explore, and we have some really precious memories from that holiday.

It almost didn't happen. Although I love flying, Sue is less enthusiastic, by which I mean this was the first time she had been on a plane, and she has a very real fear of flying that presented an almost insurmountable challenge for that holiday. We didn't fly again as a family for over 25 years, and in that time the fear of flying had grown.

That was when our son decided to get married. In Florida. Well there was no way that we weren't going to be at that wedding, and there was no way we could get there from the UK without flying, so this wedding was one PRIZE that involved a Next Exciting Win with a significant terror barrier to be overcome for Sue.

"Despite my fear of enclosed spaces, and of flying, there was no way I wasn't going to attempt the journey to be at my son's wedding, even if I didn't make it one piece."
~ Sue Fairhead

Some years previously I had taken up cycling and spent many hours in the saddle every week, and a great piece of advice I was given regarding cycling on the roads around where I live was:

"When you see a pothole, DON'T look at it! Look at the part of the road you do want to ride on, not the part you don't want to ride on."

There is some great advice here when tackling any task, and that is to focus on the excitement in a task, not on the monotony of a task. If it's helpful we can think of extrinsic and intrinsic rewards. Extrinsic rewards would be finding ways to reward yourself for having completed a dull task. Intrinsic rewards would be to focus on finding ways to make boring tasks exciting, or at least feel exciting by linking them to exciting outcomes.

For example, I am currently working on losing some excess weight (again). I could try and find non-calorific ways to reward myself for eating less or eating more healthily, or I could find ways to make eating less and eating healthily more exciting. Without doubt, the latter approach is the most effective. My approach in doing something NEW and finding my Next Exciting Win includes visualising what I might look like and how I might feel when I have lost some weight, and embracing that "not full" feeling of being slightly hungry and enjoying the exciting idea that it is in those times that I am actually shedding weight.

I conjure up a mental picture of the "food technician" in my stomach having to either store food reserves in the energy archives (when I am feeling full) or fetching food reserves from the energy archive (when I am feeling peckish). The more I can "feel peckish" the more food is fetched from the energy archive and as a result I will lose weight. This is certainly in the Inspiration Zone, and it works for me!

I am currently on a journey towards a PRIZE that involves public speaking. Having embarked on a journey to become accredited as a Certified Member of the John Maxwell Team of Speakers, Trainers and Coaches there are several challenges to overcome that are quite definitely in the Inspiration Zone. One of these challenges involves Public Speaking.

As I write this book I am part way through that particular journey, and I have used several Next Exciting Wins to move towards the PRIZE, with more to come before I get there. After working through the coaching videos and other related materials it was time to start practicing the craft. The Maxwell Method calls that "getting good".

I set out a path with a series to Next Exciting Wins to move towards that goal. These NEW tasks involved joining the Professional Speakers Association, and then delivering a presentation before a room full of Professional Speakers to obtain their feedback, and has led to signing up to enter the annual Speaker Factor competition with regional heats in the months leading up to that. Each of these talks has provided me with a NEW that was in the Inspiration Zone, each taking me beyond the Fear Barrier, and leading towards the PRIZE of becoming a Professional Speaker.

So What!

So what three things stood out to you most in this chapter?

So what is the first thing you want to share with someone else?

So what is one thing you plan to do differently?

So what NEW thing could you achieve in the next six weeks?

PART TWO

DELIVER

If leadership is taking people on a journey from here to there ...

How will you get there?

Do you get what you're hoping for?
When you look behind you, there's no open door.

Chapter 3

Influence

Recently I met up with a friend named Tony Lynch for lunch in London, and we found ourselves in an establishment called "The Wellington Hotel", which was located just across the road from Waterloo Station. It caused a moment of amusement when we briefly remembered the Battle of Waterloo and the role of the Duke of Wellington and his fellow combatants who routed Napoleon some 200 years ago in 1815.

The station also shares its name with the title of a song performed by a hitherto little known Swedish band as a representative of their country at the Eurovision Song Contest in the '70s, and they became an international success overnight. After some years at the top of the charts however their popularity started to wane, and suddenly it was "uncool" to acknowledge that you liked anything Abba related. After a few more years they became fashionable again, and soon Abba tribute bands were emerging all around! Evidently, some strong influences were around to cause a musical talent to meander between such highs and lows of popularity.

It is interesting to see how popular culture can have such an enormous influence on the fortunes of a band, and fascinating to see the impact it can have on the careers of those affected.

There are few career choices that are more demanding and challenging than those found in leading a country. Now, although I wouldn't claim to be either a politician or an authority on politics, as an interested observer the current political environment seems to offer some fascinating observations on the question of leadership and influence.

As I write this book the current leader of the left wing Labour Party in the UK, Jeremy Corbyn has introduced us to a new and curious dynamic of influence, and one that seems to have his party confused in how to respond.

At the close of the 20th Century, a charismatic young Tony Blair swept to power on a new wave of influence, with "New Labour" having taken the centre ground of politics after nearly 20 years of conservative government. Although finding himself vilified by many today, while he was in power he was a hugely influential Prime Minster in many ways. After his 10 years as the British Premier, he resigned in 2007 and he was followed by his Chancellor Gordon Brown, who although very competent was unable to demonstrate any significant influence on a country soon to be gripped by a financial crisis and was defeated at the next election.

Since then the Labour party seems to have been having trouble finding its identity, with several leaders taking it back to the more traditional left-wing roots of the party. This brings us back to the most recent of these, and the current leader of the Labour Party, Jeremy Corbyn. An article from the BBC stated:

Jeremy Corbyn's election in September 2015 as Labour leader, at the age of 66, counted as one of the biggest upsets in British political history.
~ Brian Wheeler

His nomination was a late addition to the ballot paper with just minutes to spare, and as he explained to the Guardian Newspaper:

"Well, Diane [Abbott] and John [McDonnell] have done it before, so it was my turn."
~ Jeremy Corbyn

He then proceeded to gain an unexpected victory with an overwhelming 59.5% of the votes cast and was elected leader of the Labour Party. His influence as a leader though was not universal with little support from his fellow Labour MPs, and when two-thirds of his shadow cabinet resigned he was forced by a vote of no confidence into another leadership contest. In this, he retained leadership of the party and increased his share of the vote to 61.8%!

His enormous influence and support with the grassroots of the party membership were clearly not shared by all the MPs in the Parliamentary Labour Party, and time will tell where his leadership of the Labour Party takes them.

Now, effectiveness in leadership has a lot to do with influence, and time will tell how the leadership issues related to the recent referendum vote by the British people to leave the European Union works out. For now, I just want us to see the enormous effect that influence has on leadership.

During his time in office Tony Blair had enormous influence. When Gordon Brown took over it seemed to me that he didn't, and Jeremy

Corbyn evidently has quite a mixed circle of influence. So, how has that affected their ability to lead?

John Maxwell asserts that: *"The true measure of leadership is influence— nothing more, nothing less."*

"The true measure of leadership is influence—nothing more, nothing less. Leadership cannot be awarded, appointed, or assigned. Influence cannot be mandated, only earned. Lack of an official title doesn't preclude you from leading, nor does having a position of authority qualify you to lead."
~ John Maxwell

The only way that anyone can lead effectively has nothing to do with position or title, and nothing to do with entrepreneurial skills or with knowledge. It has everything to do with their ability to influence the people that they are to lead.

"He who thinks he leads, but has no followers, is only taking a walk"
~ John Maxwell

What are your strengths, and what are the factors that you use to persuade people to follow you? What do you need to do to use your strengths to their best advantage to gain influence, and what are the factors that you struggle with that hold you back and need to be reinforced?

Pareto Priorities

I have to confess that I've never arrived at the end of the week to find that "I totally forgot to eat this week". Somehow, I always find the time to eat. Nor do I find that I have totally overlooked sleeping. Now that's not so say that sleep and diet don't get neglected somewhat from time to time, but they usually get some kind of attention every week one way or another. Usually, sometime during everyone's week, they become high enough on the list of priorities that they get added to the list of things to do today.

Dr. Stephen Covey talks about this in his well-known classic "7 Habits of Highly Effective People" as the habit of "Putting First Things First". Here he talks about putting the big rocks into your schedule first, the important things that must be done, before fitting in the other less important although often urgent tasks.

The point is well illustrated using a glass jar, and when the big rocks are put in first, then smaller pieces of gravel can fill some of the gaps, then there is still room for sand to fill more gaps, and finally, water can be poured into the jar too, before it becomes full. It'll only all fit in by starting with the big rocks first. Put the sand and water in first and there's insufficient room for the big rocks to be added to the jar.

If you don't put the big rocks in first, you'll never get them in at all.
~ Dr. Stephen Covey

When trying to figure out what is a big rock, in practice, we get help using the Pareto Principle, or the 80/20 rule. This states that you get 80% of your results from 20% of your effort. It is a principle that is used quite widely wherever you read about priorities. But where did it come from?

I first encountered this principle when I was working for a major international Tyre Manufacturer, that was apparently hitting hard times. As a result, there we had a company-wide initiative to train every employee on the Total Quality Management principles promoted by Joseph Juran (1904-2008). Juran was one of several quality gurus that emerged around this time, including people such as Philip Crosby, and Taiichi Ohno who was the architect of the Toyota Production System.

Juran encouraged his readers to focus on employing Quality by Design to replace Quality after Design; to build Quality into the product rather than performing quality control after manufacture to identify the reject products.

In particular he addressed "the vital few and the trivial many" things that had an influence on product quality and introduced "Quality Circles" to address the plethora of seemingly unimportant things (the trivial many) that can have an adverse effect on the overall quality of output. He also introduced the really helpful idea that the "Cost of Quality" can be monitored, and this was made up from the sum of the Price of Conformance plus the Price of Non-conformance.

The vital few were the few major issues that had an impact on the manufacturing process, and were addressed by forming a team of company experts to bring their minds to bear on the problem. The trivial many were lots and lots of seemingly trivial issues that would annoy the workers and staff, yet were left untreated for years on end. He used the so called Pareto Principle to distinguish between these two categories.

Now Vilfredo Pareto (1848-1923) was an Italian engineer, sociologist, economist, political scientist, and philosopher, and he coined the Pareto Principle, built on observations of his such as that 80% of the land in Italy was owned by about 20% of the population. This principle was then observed to ring true in other areas of life, and in particular, Juran used it to help identify the Vital Few things, the 20% of the causes that generated 80% of a problem. This was one of the main threads of his work and the place where he suggested that key management attention would need to be focused. He added to that by encouraging the formation of Quality Circles to address the other 80% of the causes - the trivial many (or later called the useful many).

We've all been given 24 hours in every day, and that's just enough.

So how should we apply that to this issue of prioritising then, this 80/20 rule? Well, a great way to do this is to consider three questions. Leaders ought to consider these three questions in seeking to identify their priorities, and consider all aspects of life's demands, not just the business aspects:

- What is required,
- What offers the greatest return, and
- What brings the greatest satisfaction.

Having assessed the answers to those three life questions a further 80/20 question to explore is to identify those things on the list identified here and see which items could be performed by someone else at least 80% as well as the leader can perform them, and these can be progressively delegated.

This should then leave the 20% of things that the Leader MUST do in order to be most effective, and these are the big rocks that must be put into the diary first.

So What!

So what three things stood out to you most in this chapter?

So what is the first thing you want to share with someone else?

So what is one thing you plan to do differently?

So what NEW thing could you achieve in the next six weeks?

Chapter 4

Interaction

When I was a child growing up one of the regular features of afternoon viewing involved answering the question: "*Which Window would it be?*". It was a popular British children's television series called *Play School* produced by the BBC, and preschoolers were presented with a film about everyday life and this was accessed by looking through a particular window.

When you think about it, we usually look at scenes of everyday life through our own windows, a view that is affected by our own culture and values. I was once standing with a friend of mine - I'll call him Steve - at a social event, and we were generally chatting and catching up on life. Observing some friends that had just arrived he asked if I knew how they were, and said something I found quite curious at the time. He said, "*don't you get a vibe about them*". I remember replying that I must be a "vibe-free zone" as I didn't get any vibes about them at all, and actually, I just wondered what he meant.

Recently I had the opportunity to explore a really helpful set of windows that explain so much of how people interact and misunderstand each other. I spent a few days with Dr Robert Rohm and his wife Alice along with several others that were interested in learning more about how personalities and behaviour styles can help to solve some "relationship puzzles" in life.

Dr. Rohm runs an organisation called *Personality Insights* and his focus is on the DISC theory originally described by William Marston and further developed by Walter Clarke, which explores four different behavioural traits that were identified by Marston as dominance, inducement, submission, and compliance. These traits were based on the four combinations available from having an outgoing or reserved personality, and an inclination towards being task focused or people focused.

Studies have shown that this model has credible scientific validity as a helpful psychometric instrument for understanding and getting to know people and their behaviour in interpersonal situations. It has also been seen to bring a very helpful insight into exploring different leadership methods and discovering which methods are more suitable for a variety of circumstances in order to help leaders to become more effective.

People who are both *outgoing and task* focused are described as **D**ominant, people who are *outgoing and people* focused are described as **I**nspiring, people that are *reserved and people* focused are described as **S**upportive, and people that are *reserved and task* focused are described as **C**autious. Of course, in the real world, all of us exhibit some combination of several of these behavioural traits, and this model gives us a really helpful way of exploring that.

The more you think about the model and the people that you know, the more it starts to help to understand what drives people's behaviour. Dr. Rohm puts it this way: "*It makes sense to check out the airspace you're flying into.*" When discussing these behaviour characteristics people seem to immediately come to mind, and then that "aha" moment comes along and with "so that's why they acted like that".

"It makes sense to check out the airspace you're flying in to."
~ Dr. Robert Rohm

In fact, Dr. Rohm explains that he was first introduced to the model when trying to understand the difficulty he had relating to his 12-year-old daughter, and since then has become an enthusiast in sharing the model with others around the world. He has developed several really useful ways of sharing the model and using it to help understand how and why people respond the way they do.

I came away from the visit with some really useful insights into my own behaviour and that of those I love, and of the those I come into contact with both socially and at work too. In fact, it provides a great way to help understand people and to related to them in a more meaningful way.

It helped me see why I came to consider myself as being a "vibe free zone" when I was chatting with that friend who described our mutual friends saying, *"don't you get a vibe about them"*. He had a very high S personality and to him, the vibe was plain as day, whereas for me it was more difficult to see. Now I know!

Helping you learn

On the day I started my consultancy business I didn't have a grand plan and design of what I wanted to do, but I did have a passion that I wanted to give a voice to. The weekend between the Friday when I was having lunch with the head of the Nuclear Industry Association to the Monday when I was launching my new business was filled with loads of ideas and opportunities and very little certainty.

The first few projects were quite a mix of activities from lecturing to undergraduates and postgraduates in Project Management and IT, to teaching teenagers how to play violin and piano. I soon settled into the main activity of delivering Sales and Marketing support to various business, along with delivering a variety of small group training courses.

The underlying passion in all of my work is that of helping people learn. I have often been heard to say at the start of a training course that "if I just teach and you don't learn then I've not done my job - since I'm not just here to teach; I'm here to help you learn".

For me that is manifest in many ways outside of the training environment, and I derive significant personal satisfaction when I hear people share something they've learned from me. Some years ago I was working alongside the leader of an organisation who shared with me that in all the years of training for his current post he hadn't had a single day of leadership training. At a result, I signed us both up for a training programme on Leadership delivered by a John Maxwell company and we attended together, and we both came away having learned some great lessons. During my time with that leader I would occasionally observe him sharing with others something that I'd helped him learn, and for me, that was a complete reward in itself.

"Great things can happen when you don't care who gets the credit."
~ Mark Twain

In a Leadership Podcast entitled "Empowering Leaders", Craig Groeschel suggests that to empower leaders we need to Communicate with Clarity & Extend Trust.

"We empower people through clarity and trust. We must be clear on the what and the why, but not the how. Trust those you empower with the how."
~ Craig Groeschel

To create an empowering culture it is important to empower leaders by finding the right people, empowering them with a clear understanding of the passion for the mission (the why), providing a clarity of their purpose and the part they can play in achieving that mission (the what), and trusting them to lead in the best way they know how.

In "*The Law of Empowerment*" John Maxwell describes the Ford Motor Company and how Henry Ford had created the world's first mass-produced motor vehicle, and how it changed the face of twentieth century American life with the Model T. However, he goes on to explain that the leadership model used by three successive generations of Fords at the helm of the company was beset by conflict and continual undermining of the senior executives. On one occasion, when a new prototype was produced by his designers, Henry Ford proceeded to rip the doors off their hinges and destroy the car with his bare hands! This controlling defensive leadership nearly took the company into bankruptcy, and at one point it was losing one million dollars a day!

Without trusting your leaders to lead in their own way, even with a clarity of purpose, the result will be fear and paralysis, and a continual struggle for growth. Once the passion for the mission and the clarity of the purpose is established and really understood by all, it is vitally important that your leaders are trusted to develop and deliver their own strategy with your full support.

"Most leaders would agree that they'd be better off having an average strategy with superb execution than a superb strategy with poor execution. Those who execute always have the upper hand."
~ Dr. Stephen Covey

For a large part of my career, I was a project manager in a company that produced control system automation projects for large construction projects in the nuclear industry. At the early stages of one such project, I was appointed as project manager shortly after the project had started, and it was in the early initial design stage. As is typical in such projects we were on a fixed price contract for delivering the project, however, the customer requirements weren't entirely clear (for genuine reasons) and for some aspects of the work, the requirements were experiencing some significant changes.

The project team that were working on this part of the project were doing their best to manage these changes and to keep on top of the work that it caused, however that meant the work wasn't getting signed off and we were encountering increased costs. So, there were a couple of directions I could go in to manage the process.

The one that I chose was to empower the team by explaining the commercial framework in such a way that they could grasp the underlying issues, and then to facilitate a discussion with them about how we could satisfy the customer's requirements without compromising the commercial position. This included accommodating the changed requirements while ensuring that any additional costs incurred in new requirements and rework associated with completed activities were accounted for and understood by the customer. In this way, I was able to support the team as they engaged with the new requirements and trust them to ensure that changes were correctly accounted for.

"The best executive is the one who has sense enough to pick good men to do what wants done, and self-restraint enough to keep from meddling with them while they do it."
~ Theodore Roosevelt

So What!

So what three things stood out to you most in this chapter?

So what is the first thing you want to share with someone else?

So what is one thing you plan to do differently?

So what NEW thing could you achieve in the next six weeks?

Chapter 5

Implementation

Have you ever experienced a time when you wanted to hum a tune; you know the song but the tune just won't come to mind? *"You know, it's the one that goes ... ermmm ... how does it go?"* Even worse is when the lyrics to another song keep clouding your mind to keep the right tune at bay.

It was a cold evening in a hall not far from where I live; the band were playing and today I was operating the sound desk. The event had taken several months in planning and preparation, not to mention practice. We had a vision for what we wanted to do that evening, we were on a mission to raise some money for our chosen charity, a very deserving cause.

Earlier that afternoon I had set about the task of dismantling the entire sound system from its usual location and rebuilding it temporarily in a new venue. Prior to that we had inspected the venue and made a note of the location of the power sockets, and we had all the equipment we needed for tonight's concert. The bar had been manned and the other refreshments had been bought and set up, tickets had been sold and everything was going according to plan.

Part way through the evening, as planned, I handed over control of the sound desk to a colleague and made my way from the back of the auditorium towards the stage, clutching my trusty electric violin. I was to be the feature for this number and join the band to play a jazz style improvised solo to accompany the vocalist, however, all I could remember was the first note I was to play. As I walked to the front of the hall all eyes seemed to turn to me, and as I stepped onto the stage the band fired up, and still all I could remember was the first note!

I played my note, and then the next came seemingly from nowhere, followed by the rest of the first line, and soon we were in full swing. Fortunately, the planning and practice paid off and no-one noticed my panic, and the piece was performed without incident.

This is when you appreciate the value of planning, preparation and practice. For the vision to become a successful reality every aspect of the plan needs to have been considered and thought through in advance.

> "A project is a unique venture with a beginning and an end, conducted by people to meet established goals within parameters of cost, schedule and quality."
> ~ Buchanan and Boddy

I have spent much of my career as a Project Manager and I know very well the need for thorough planning to achieve a successful outcome to a project, since I have also spent several years as a Trustee and Director of the Association for Project Management (APM).

The concept of Project Management as a discipline was developed for managing the US space program in the early 1960's and its practice has expanded rapidly since then. In the UK, the APM has been instrumental in developing the profession of Project Management with the development of the "Body of Knowledge" that all Project Management professionals would be expected to know, and they now offer Chartered Engineer status for the Project Management profession.

John Maxwell refers to this as **"The Law of Navigation"** in the 21 Irrefutable Laws of Leadership which states that leaders "... *have a vision for their destination, understand what's required to get there, and know whom they need on the team to be successful."*

"Anyone can steer the ship, but it takes a leader to chart the course. Leaders keep an eye on the future, scanning the horizon for indications of which course appears the best. Then, based on what they see, they set the direction for the organisation."
~ **John Maxwell**

6S Implementation Framework

A helpful framework to use when developing a project is to consider the **6S Implementation Framework** which is used to develop a **Project Management Plan**.

The Project Management Plan is at the heart of the 6S Implementation framework and it examines all six elements described in this section in turn to come up with a comprehensive plan for effective formation, mobilisation, monitoring, management and deployment of a project.

6S Implementation Framework

Spend	*how much will it cost?*
Specification	*what will it look like?*
Schedule	*when is it needed by?*
Staff	*people working on the project*
Stakeholders	*people affected by the project*
Speculation	*what could go wrong, or go right?*

This looks first at the outcome aspects of Cost, Quality and Time, usually shown as a triangle to illustrate their interdependence, and initially developed in the mid-1980s by Dr. Martin Barnes. These are the first three S-Factors of Spend, Specification and Schedule.

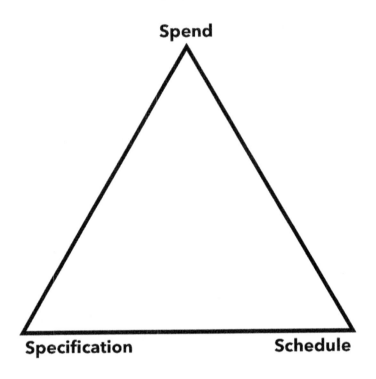

Spend

Specification   **Schedule**

*The triangle demonstrates that quality, cost and time
(Specification, Spend and Schedule) are interrelated.
Focusing or fixing one point of the triangle impacts the
other two points.*
~ Dennis Lock

There are many tried and trusted techniques available to help with
monitoring and control of these three factors, and the development of
a Project Management Plan is helpful to document and record these
plans as they evolve. Work Breakdown Structures and Cost Breakdown
Structures, along with a clear definition of the desired deliverable
outcomes are all necessary elements to produce a plan that has a good
chance of producing the desired results.

> *"If the leader can't navigate the people through rough waters, he is liable to sink the ship ... In the end, it's not the size of the project that determines its acceptance, support and success. It's the size of the leader."*
> **~ John Maxwell**

These three S-factors of Spend, Specification and Schedule can each be monitored and managed, but none can be controlled in isolation. Changes to any one of these factors will inevitably have an impact on the other two.

> *You manage things, you lead people. We went overboard on management and forgot about leadership. It might help if we ran the MBAs out of Washington.*
> **~ Rear Admiral Grace Hopper**

The next two S-factors to be considered are both people factors, from the perspective of Staff working on the project, and of the Stakeholders, i.e. all the people that will be effected in any way by the project. We have looked at some of these people issues already in this book, and they are developed further in the 6S Implementation Framework.

The last factor to be considered in developing a complete Project Management Plan is that of Speculation. This covers firstly all of the things that might go wrong with the project, the risks, and addresses each one in turn to mitigate the risks. It then goes on to consider all of the things that might go right, and yield some kind of advantage.

The 6S **Risk Management Process** includes three stages of:

- **Risk Identification** – the **chance** of diverse consequences or loss occurring,

- **Risk Assessment** – the probability or **likelihood** of the risk occurring,
- **Risk Mitigation** – what to do about it,

Working through this process will result in a Residual Risk, which then has the **6S CARAT** framework applied to each risk in turn. For this each risk is considered and consigned to one of the following categories which are also explored further in the 6S Implementation Framework.

- **Contingency Plan** – develop a plan to use in the event that this risk occurs
- **Avoid** – do something differently so that the risk is avoided
- **Reduce** – find a way of reducing the risk so that the impact is reduced to a minimum
- **Accept** – simply accept that the risk may occur and deal with it if that happens, and finally
- **Transfer** – this usually involves some form of sub-contract work, or insurance policy.

When you have developed the "All goes to plan" plan in your Project Management Plan, considered all the options and risks, and invested in your people, you need to remember that plans are made to be changed. All project plans need regular mid-course corrections to stay on track and deliver the vision they were designed to fulfil.

What skills, experience and training do you have that will support the delivery of a successful project outcome? What are your strengths, and where are your weaknesses? In developing the plan to deliver your vision, make sure to consider who else you need to have on board for the journey. It's team-work that makes the dream work!

So What!

So what three things stood out to you most in this chapter?

So what is the first thing you want to share with someone else?

So what is one thing you plan to do differently?

So what NEW thing could you achieve in the next six weeks?

PART THREE

DEVELOP

If leadership is taking people on a journey from here to there ...

Where next?

Now looking back at all we've planned,
We let so many dreams just slip through our hands.

Chapter 6

Increase

Everything I've touched I've taught. Well, not quite everything - there are some things that many of my friends are glad that I avoid, like singing and cooking.

The author Robert Louis Stevenson once said: "*I consider the success of my day based on the seeds I sow, not the harvest I reap.*" and that's a saying worthy of some thought and reflection. Rather than focusing on income, maybe we could focus some energy on investment, of time.

"*I would rather have it said, 'he lived usefully' than 'he died rich'.*"
~ *Benjamin Franklin.*

In 2016 I was a participant in a self-development program that focused on finding your purpose in life. It was an online webinar, and to be honest I attended initially more out of an interest in the technology and teaching method than of the content, however before the event had even started I was invited to lead a breakout group, and then to deliver one of the sessions.

The topics that the program covered were to help you to identify your personal strengths and values, and combine those with the lessons learned from your personal timeline. I found the contribution from my personal timeline to be a fairly unusual element in the process, and actually one that revealed an interesting feature for me.

I noticed that over the years I have found myself professionally teaching a number of diverse topics including ice-skating, skiing, cycling, violin, piano, guitar, IT, project management, leadership and personal effectiveness. History has taught me that whatever I become interested in learning, becomes an avenue to help others to learn too. I also discovered that one of the best ways to learn any subject is to teach it to others!

I remember becoming interested in leadership topics when I was a frequent traveler with work, as I was spending quite a lot of time in stations and airport lounges. It started off as a casual interest, and then became more focused as my work involved leading larger teams, mainly in a project management role delivering control system refurbishment projects for the UK nuclear industry, and later when I launched my own business.

One particular project in the voluntary sector took my interest some years ago and remains an ongoing passion. It has resulted in my involvement over several years in the leadership team for an online community with some 600 volunteers in 40 countries.

"It's not the years in your life, it's the life in your years"

It was the combination of these two threads from my personal interests and timeline that were coming together to point to a new direction that was to emerge for me and has become a particular passion and purpose. I was reminded of a quote that said: "*It's not the years in your life, it's the life in your years*" and for me, that resonated with this newly identified purpose in life.

John Maxwell calls this "The Law of Contribution" in his book "The 15 Invaluable Laws of Growth" where he observes "*If you're not doing something with your life, it doesn't matter how long it is!*". It turns out that am not alone in finding personal fulfilment in helping others learn from my journey, and I have found that my greatest reward comes from knowing that others have found value in something I have shared.

> "*We are like dwarfs sitting on the shoulders of giants. We see more, and things that are more distant, than they did, not because our sight is superior or because we are taller than they, but because they raise us up, and by their great stature add to ours.*"
> ~ **John of Salisbury**

I am fortunate enough to have learned from those that have gone before me. From some I have learned through reading their books, from others it was the talks they have delivered or from online learning platforms. In many cases, I have been able to learn by putting ideas from other people into practice, and in other cases, I have been able to learn from the mistakes that I have made along the way. Oftentimes it is the mistakes that have yielded the best learning experiences and certainly the most memorable.

History is bunk

History. "The only thing you can do with a history degree, is teach it to students." Well, that's what I thought as a young engineering graduate.

It's interesting how your views can change, and in the last couple of years, I've spent many a happy hour discovering how lessons from history can help inform decisions today.

"You all remember," said the Controller, in his strong deep voice, "you all remember, I suppose, that beautiful and inspired saying of Our Ford's: History is bunk. History," he repeated slowly, "is bunk."
Mustapha Mond *in*
Aldous Huxley's Brave New World

It's fascinating how a subject, once considered boring, useless and lifeless can turn into a topic of fascination and inspiration. My curiosity to learn a little more about European History was sparked by a rather impulsive purchase of an old book entitled "*The Story of America: A National Geographic Picture Atlas*" from a second-hand store in Oklahoma. I thoroughly enjoyed reading about the history of America which enriched my understanding of the origins of the nation and gave me a whole new interest in exploring new places whenever we manage to make a visit there.

This also generated an interest in the European history that led up to the origins of the USA as we know it today, especially around the Boston Tea Party of 1773. That led on to a continuing interest in a subject once thought of as boring and irrelevant.

One of the things I noticed is that history is littered with people falling out with other people, often because of misunderstandings or differences in culture, and going to war because of that. It seems that we are really quite good at falling out with people that we don't understand. It also seems that history is marked by long seasons of things remaining the same, interspersed with short bouts of upheaval where there is a significant change.

The interest in history also led onto a fascinating journey of exploration of personal purpose and direction. One of the results of that journey involved exploring the question "what works" with regard to life and career. I was encouraged to explore my personal timeline to see what my personal history could teach me about myself, and about my interests, skills and values. It also led to a challenge which can be summed up in the words of Robert Schuller who said:

"What would you attempt if you knew you couldn't fail."
~ Robert Schuller

Well, one way of discovering what I could do without failing was to see what I had done that hadn't failed! My personal history timeline gave some very clear indications where those strengths lay and led to a personal reassessment process.

One of the outcomes of that reassessment was to discover a capacity for new activities that I didn't know was possible. It turns out that the statement that "most experts believe that people typically use only 10% of their true potential" isn't actually true, however, what is true is that we are capable of far more than we know. There's a rule called the

40% rule, and this states that "when your mind is telling you you're done, you're really only 40% done", and this seems to have evidence to back it up.

"When your mind is telling you you're done, you're really only 40% done"
~ Jesse Itzler

It turns out that most people seem to hit a wall that can be found less than half the way to their actual capacity, and at that point, it seems like they can't go on. For most people, however, they are able to go on well beyond that limit they just don't know it. When that's combined with one of the major stumbling blocks to be found preventing productivity at work, the truth is that there is a whole lot more that could be accomplished than is actually achieved.

One of the reasons for that lack of productivity is that we are often called on to work in areas where we are not using our strengths. When we are in our strength zone we are able to deliver at a significantly higher level than when we are working outside of it. Think of a basketball player trying to be a horse jockey, or a wrestler trying to be a long distance runner, and you'll see athletes working outside their strength zone. It seems so obvious in the world of athletics, yet we do it all the time at work!

"Learning is discovering that something is possible."
~ Fritz Perls

The key to achieving more is to stop thinking "more work" and start figuring out "what works". More work won't increase your capacity, it will just result in more work! To increase your capacity you need to do more of what works and less of what doesn't. John Maxwell explains in the Law of Expansion that it needs a change of language from "Can I?" to "How can I?". It means no longer exploring the world of *more work*, and instead, making an assumption that there is another way, and that we just need to find it. Once we make that transition we are able to grow and thus keep on increasing our capacity!

"Man's mind, once stretched by a new idea, never regains its original dimensions."
~ Oliver Wendell Holmes

There ain't no rules around here

The first time I visited Cartagena in Spain with some friends I had a fascinating tour around the ancient Roman Theatre there. However, the second time I made that visit was so much more rewarding.

The reason? In the intervening couple of years, I had taken an interest in European History, and learning to speak Spanish. What a difference that made!

"I have no special talents. I am only passionately curious."
~ Albert Einstein

My curiosity to learn a little more about European History was initiated by a rather impulsive purchase of an old book on American History, that sparked an interest in history generally, and led on to an interest in European history, and to learning about the background to the building of the Roman Theatre in Cartagena. Along with my elementary skills in learning Spanish this meant that on my second visit to the area I was able to tie together the history with a limited understanding of the descriptions of the exhibits in the museum and a whole new world of exploration, curiosity and interest had been born.

Now the fascinating thing about that episode is that I had absolutely no interest in either history or languages when I was younger. It is so interesting how a small dose of curiosity can make such an enormous difference not only in what we find interesting and how we spend our time, but how much more interesting and enriching other activities can become as a result.

The single greatest difference between curious, growing people and those who aren't is the belief that they can learn, grow and change.
*~ **John Maxwell***

When I started out in the world of business I was employed by a firm that had several factories in the UK and Europe, and my job took me to visit many of them quite regularly. The net result was that now and again I found myself in airports with time to spare, and as I've described above that was when I started to find an interest in the work by Peter Drucker, Ken Blanchard and John Maxwell among others.

"My greatest strength as a consultant is to be ignorant and ask a few questions."
*~ **Peter Drucker***

It also led to an enduring interest in the topic of Leadership, and of learning about what it takes to make a great leader, and indeed to ask "what is leadership" and what difference does it make. At the time I was a Project Manager and it was really interesting to see the difference leadership can make on the way a project turns out. It was then that I learned that "you can manage things, but you need to lead people".

At the time I was involved in costing up control system automation projects and then delivering the projects that we were successful in winning. In a world where the margins are around 10%, it was really easy to be just a little too expensive and lose the business, or be a little too cheap, win the business and make a loss! It was here that I learned the benefit of what John Maxwell calls "the Law of Curiosity" since the best way to succeed in that world was to find an innovative way to make a great solution at a lower cost.

> *"When average people ask themselves, "Can I do this?" they base it on the circumstances they see.... An abundant thinker asks, "How can I?" This simple twist of semantics changes everything. It forces your mind to create a new solution.*
> *~ Brian Klemmer*

In the initial stages of putting a solution together, it was imperative that we spent some time on the "How can I?" question to look for all the ways that we could deliver a solution to satisfy the specification and yet take cost out of the process. It was all too easy to come up with the same ways of providing a solution as everyone else, the secret to successful tendering was to find a way of delivering the same outcome in new, innovative ways.

> *Almost every advance in art, cooking, medicine, agriculture, engineering, marketing, politics, education, and design has occurred when someone challenged the rules and tried another approach.*
> *~ Roger von Oech*

That principle remains so true in the effective Leadership of any organisation, and never has it been truer than in today's information overloaded world. Thomas Edison was always trying to innovate and come up with new ideas, perhaps the best known of which include the phonograph, and motion picture camera and the incandescent electric light bulb. He famously said: *"There ain't no rules around here! We're trying to accomplish something!"* and *"I have not failed. I've just found 10,000 ways that won't work."*

Be prepared

"It's character forming." I remember someone saying that to me, and somehow whenever it applies it never seems to help! It certainly didn't at the time, since I had found myself managing a Power Station control system refurbishment project that was experiencing a series of challenges in the last few weeks as we approached go-live.

As we ascend the ladder of personal growth there are a number of rungs that we'll need to climb, that if missed on the way up will be sure to cause our downfall later on.

"Ninety-nine percent of leadership failures are failures of character."
~ Norman Schwarzkopf

Author Stephen Covey writes about the difference between Character and Personality in driving personal success, especially in leaders. He suggests that until around 100 years ago the Character Ethic was the main driver and that in the years since then it has gradually shifted to a Personality Ethic, which is more dependent on self-belief and observed performance.

We can see examples all around us of people that have "made it", only to fall from grace due to some apparent moral failing or another. Many well-known examples in the world of the media and politics fill the papers and the casual conversations with all too much frequency. They leave a lesson that we would be well served in learning even if we don't frequent the world of media or politics, as we diligently work on personal growth.

> "If you're not careful, your talent will take you places that your character can't keep you."
> ~ **Eric Thomas**

Character doesn't just have to do with moral judgements, but it can also have to do with culture too. Things that one culture consider to be appropriate can seem quite inappropriate to another culture. This can be observed in the world of politics in recent years in the UK and brings a fascinating perspective to view.

In recent years the fate of our country's leaders has taken some interesting turns, and one aspect is that of the leader who takes over following the resignation of a Prime Minister. John Major, Gordon Brown and Theresa May all found themselves in the hot seat without the benefit of a General Election victory to get them there, and I wonder if we can see a common thread.

By that, I mean that the journey these three politicians took involved a vote by their political colleagues alone, without the intervention of the electorate. Now I don't wish to make any kind of political or moral statement here, but rather to draw out the fact that in our terms - for those of us not in such public office - they were appointed not elected, they were put into place by a process that was not the normal process that they would soon have to experience to stay in office. They were judged fit or otherwise using criteria that were quite different to those which they would have to face to keep them there.

Although it is too early to say what will actually happen for Theresa May, the other two politicians found the "normal" process of a General Election somewhat more difficult and challenging than the election by their peers. I am intrigued by this as it impacts on the topic of leadership since these people are appointed to one of the highest positions of leadership in our country. The standards and values by which they are judged and appointed or elected are quite different for each constituency.

"The life of every man is a diary in which he means to write one story, and writes another; and his humblest hour is when he compares the volume as it is with what he vowed to make it."
~ J.M. Barrie

The Law of the Farm says that you can't reap in the fall without planting in the spring and watering during the summer. Senator Dan Coats once said, *"Character cannot be summoned at the moment of crisis if it has been squandered by years of compromise and rationalisation."* On our journey up the ladder of personal growth, it is important to ensure that the proper foundations are in place in order that the growth achieved is sustainable in the longer term.

Habits are at the core of making firm foundations, and making sure to build intentional habits (and intentionally avoiding others) will have a significant impact on the longevity of a journey, and a leadership journey is no different.

Achievement to most people is something you do ... to the high achiever, it is something you are."
~ Doug Firebaugh.

Collateral Beauty

The other week I was discussing the plot of a film entitled "*Collateral Beauty*" with some friends, and although I didn't pay too much attention to the detailed plot as I was watching the film there was an interesting truth that seemed to emerge as we discussed our recollections.

"You've been given a gift, this profound connection to everything. Just look for it, and I promise you it's there, the collateral beauty."
~ Allan Loeb (Collateral Beauty)

This was the idea that the pain of a tragic loss can reveal a beauty that would otherwise probably have remained hidden. That's not to say that the loss was in itself a thing of beauty, or that the pain could in any way become less painful, but rather that something of beauty can often be revealed that is only found as a result of the loss.

"I'm in all of it. I'm the darkness and the light, I'm the sunshine and the storm. Yes, you're right, I was there in her laugh, but I'm also here now in your pain. I'm the reason for everything. I am the only "why." Don't try and live without me, Howard. Please don't."
~ ibid

No pain, no gain. So goes the well-known saying, and it usually refers to the refrain used by athletes which says they need to endure pain to achieve professional excellence. From my time as a sports coach I know that most effective muscular growth occurs during the last one or two repetitions of an exercise. The initial reps are really only there to fatigue the muscles and the last painful reps are the most effective in eliciting growth.

A similar principle seems to be at work in other areas of life too. So often there is a choice between the pleasure of indulgence accompanied with the pain of regret - or the pain of self-discipline which brings the pleasure of achievement. I know this particularly well since I am in the middle of a weight loss program, and my weakness is, well, food. Apparently I have an overactive knife and fork! It's only when I can contain my self-indulgence and substitute it for self-discipline that I see any results.

When painful and difficult times come around, and they surely do, it is how we deal with them that makes the difference. When pursuing a prize there is often a pain to be endured, and that is where self-discipline can bring the prize within reach.

"Success in life comes not from holding a good hand, but in playing a poor hand well."
~ **Warren G Lester**

Some years ago, I was having lunch with the head of the British Nuclear Industry Forum in my capacity as Sales Engineer for an Automation and Control Systems company. We were one of the main suppliers of automation and control systems to the Nuclear Industry in the UK and this was a key contact, and I had just landed an enquiry for one of the largest refurbishment projects at a Nuclear Power Station we had ever tendered for.

Coming back to the scene I described in the preface, when I returned to the office after lunch with a customer I was invited for a discussion with the MD to learn that the company had decided to cut back on our work in this sector, and that my job was no longer required - I was to be offered my previous job back as a Project Manager, or I could take a voluntary redundancy.

That started a period of intensely challenging times as I had decided that I wanted to move on from the world of Project Management, and I took the painful road towards self-employment with no idea what I might actually do. It would be true to say that I had many times when I regretted that decision and decided what a reckless fool I had been, to have turned away from a secure position in a company within which I had worked very successfully for over 10 years.

The very real pain experienced in setting out on such a new, different and unexpected path was very real at the time and very relevant to this topic.

I am reminded of the story of an acclaimed pianist who was chatting with someone from the audience after a show who remarked "I would do anything to be able to play like you." Their response was something like: "No you wouldn't; you wouldn't want to practice for 8 hours every day, 7 days a week for years, and give up everything else just to have the possibility of performing." So how much do we want our prize? How much are we actually prepared to sacrifice to achieve it?

If we can embrace our prize, embrace the self-discipline to persevere in our pursuit of the prize, then we will have a much greater chance of actually achieving the result.

"Life is not the way it's supposed to be. It's the way it is. The way you cope with it is what makes the difference."
~ **Virginia Satir**

So What!

So what three things stood out to you most in this chapter?

So what is the first thing you want to share with someone else?

So what is one thing you plan to do differently?

So what NEW thing could you achieve in the next six weeks?

ABOUT THE AUTHOR

Roger is a leadership specialist delivering Leadership for Business Achievement through Speaking, Coaching and Training for business leaders and entrepreneurs. He is a certified by the John Maxwell Team and the Personality Insights Institute.

"He is articulate, tracks complex issues with ease and has an incredible gift for raising pearls of wisdom out of the murky depths of people and process." His passion is to help people to learn effective leadership skills, to lead their teams to capitalize on their strengths and passions, to realize their dreams.

Leadership for Business also invests into the dreams of families in the world's underserved communities to offer them small loans that empower them to invest in their future, to provide for their families and give back to their communities.

Printed in Great Britain
by Amazon